The Bartholomew Children's World Atlas

A book of maps for young children

Jacqueline Tivers and Michael Day

John Bartholomew & Son Limited, Edinburgh

Introducing Simon and Sarah

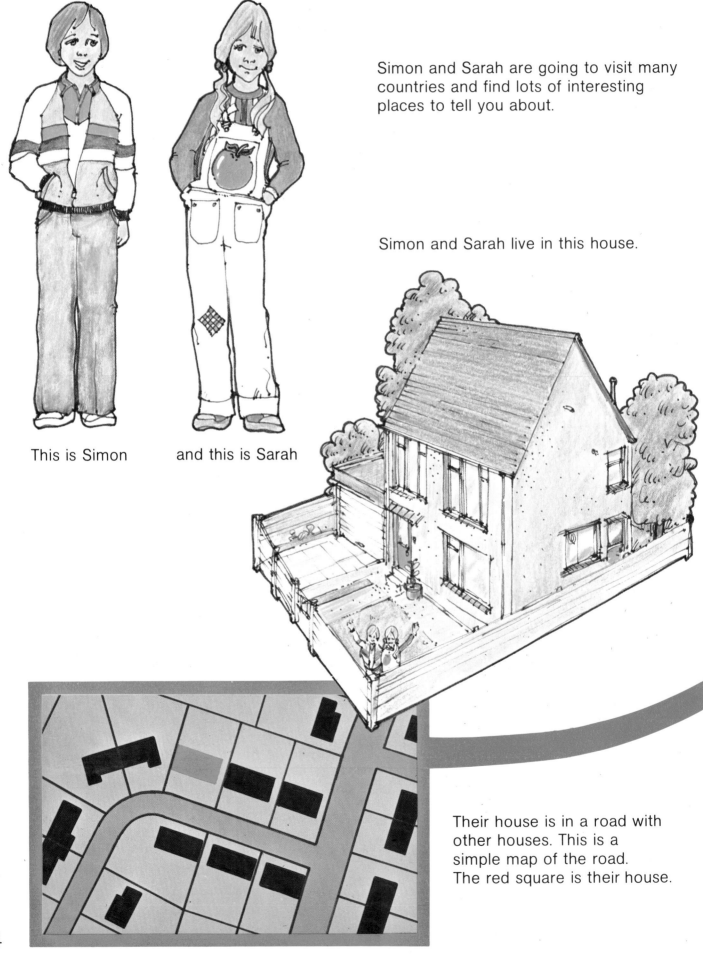

Simon and Sarah are going to visit many countries and find lots of interesting places to tell you about.

This is Simon   and this is Sarah

Simon and Sarah live in this house.

Their house is in a road with other houses. This is a simple map of the road. The red square is their house.

The road they live in is part of a town. The town has a large number of roads and a lot of houses. Can you find the red dot which shows where Simon and Sarah live?

Their town is in Great Britain, which is a small country in the world. The red dot shows where the town is on this map. You can see from this map that Great Britain is an island and is surrounded by sea. Can you find this island on the map on pages 6 and 7? On pages 10 and 11 is a bigger map of Great Britain.

World Map

We can see Great Britain, the country where Simon and Sarah live, on this map of the world.

On this map it is shaded red.

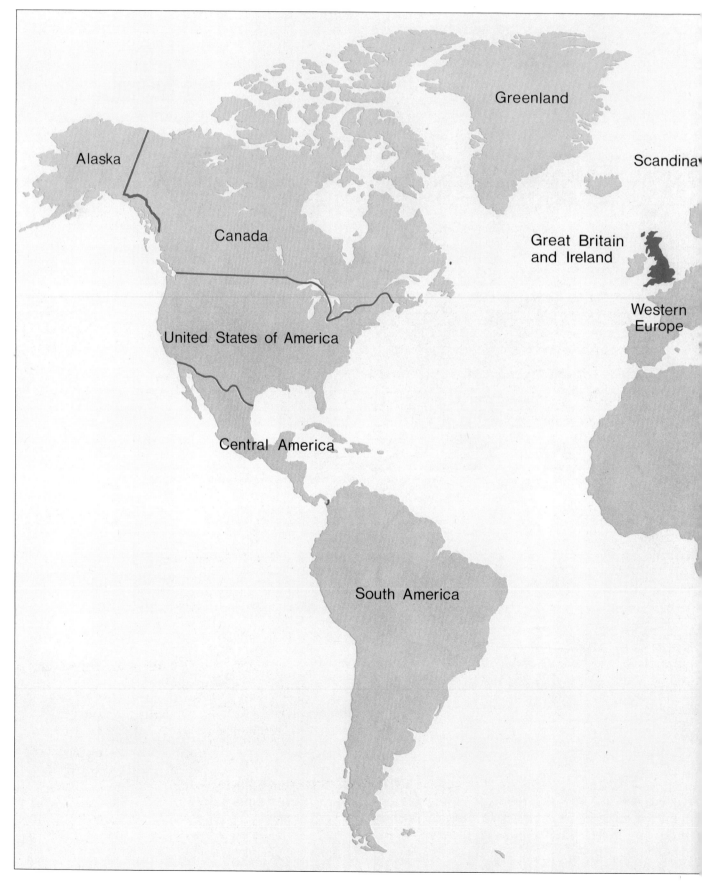

Alaska

Canada

Greenland

Scandina

United States of America

Great Britain and Ireland

Western Europe

Central America

South America

Each part of the world that Simon and Sarah are going to visit is shown too.

On every page of the book you will find a small map of the world showing the area that Simon and Sarah are visiting shaded red.

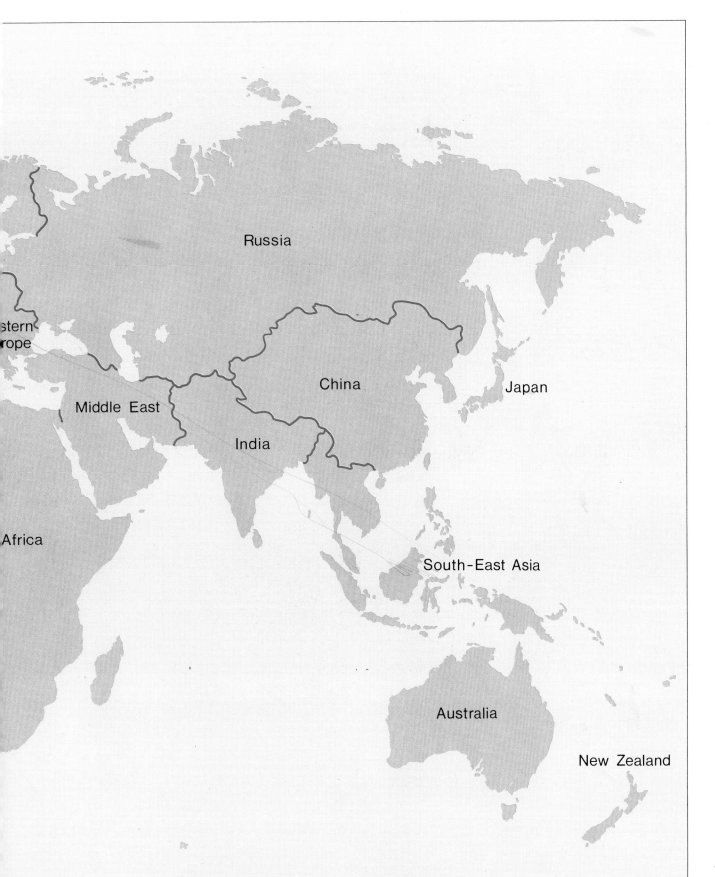

Russia

stern rope

Middle East

China

Japan

India

Africa

South-East Asia

Australia

New Zealand

Of course, the continents of the world are not really blank as they appear on the last map. Some parts of the world are covered with thick forests. Other parts are desert or farmland. In some areas there are high mountains and deep valleys. As Simon and Sarah travel around the world they will see all these different types of land, and the maps of the places they visit will be shaded in different colours.

Grassland  Forest

Farmland  Mountains

Desert  Tundra

Simon and Sarah will also see some of the things people do in the countries they visit. The symbols on the maps will show where people work, the crops they grow, and the animals they keep.

These are the symbols you will find on the maps.

The crops people grow

- timber
- wheat and barley
- maize
- rice
- potatoes or yams
- peanuts or groundnuts
- apples and pears
- oranges and lemons
- grapes
- bananas
- dates
- sugar
- coffee

- tea
- cocoa
- cotton
- rubber
- tobacco
- palm oil

The animals people keep

- cows (Europe and America)
- cows (Africa and Asia)
- sheep (Europe and Australia)
- sheep (Africa and Asia)
- pigs

Where people work

- offices
- factories
- mining
- coal mining
- oil and gas
- nuclear power
- sea port
- fishing port

Places for holidays

- beach holidays
- skiing holidays
- walking holidays

Look for Simon and Sarah on every page and see what they are doing in each part of the world.

On most pages you will also find some wild animal symbols. These show where those animals live.

9

Great Britain and Ireland

People have lived here for thousands of years. There are many ruins of old houses and forts. Britain was the first country to have factories. Most families live in towns, but there are lots of small villages.

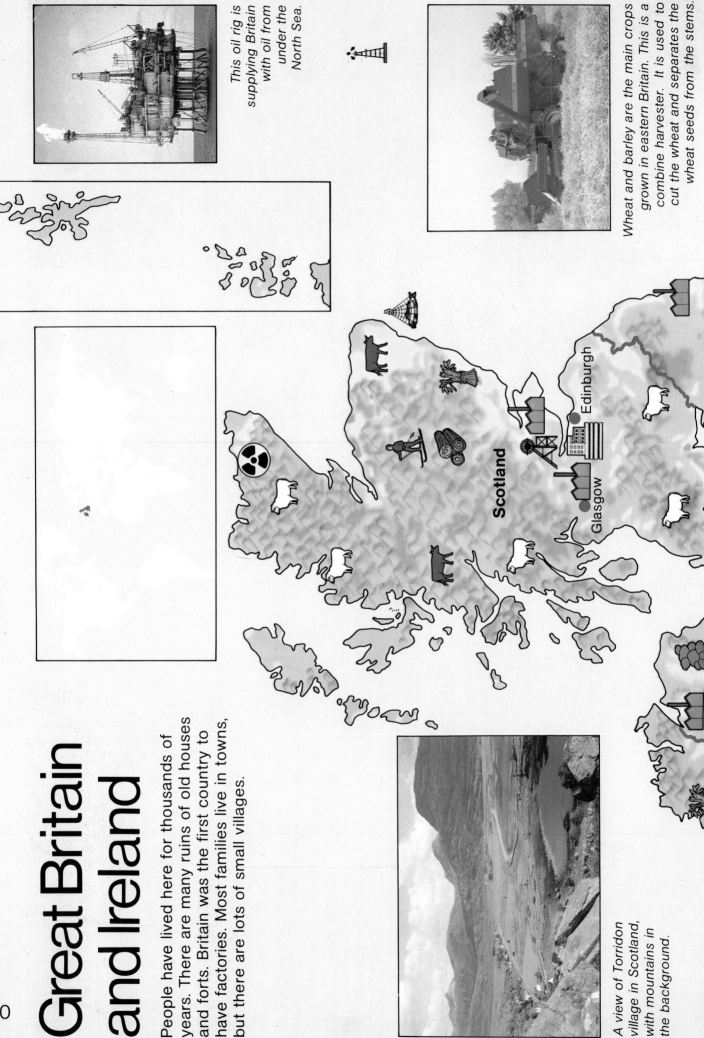

This oil rig is supplying Britain with oil from under the North Sea.

Wheat and barley are the main crops grown in eastern Britain. This is a combine harvester. It is used to cut the wheat and separates the wheat seeds from the stems.

Scotland

Edinburgh

Glasgow

A view of Torridon village in Scotland, with mountains in the background.

England

Manchester

Birmingham

Wales

Cardiff

London

Thames

Ireland

Dublin

This is an English village called Shaftesbury in Dorset.

Part of the Irish coast.

This is Pembroke Castle in Wales. It was built about the year 1200.

11

Western Europe

There are many areas with lots of factories. Near the coast big steel works and oil refineries have been built, but in the mountains the factories are smaller. In Switzerland watches and clocks are made and the Swiss have become famous as manufacturers of good watches. Because the south of Europe is warm and sunny, grapes and other fruit can be grown. The coast of southern Europe is a popular holiday area.

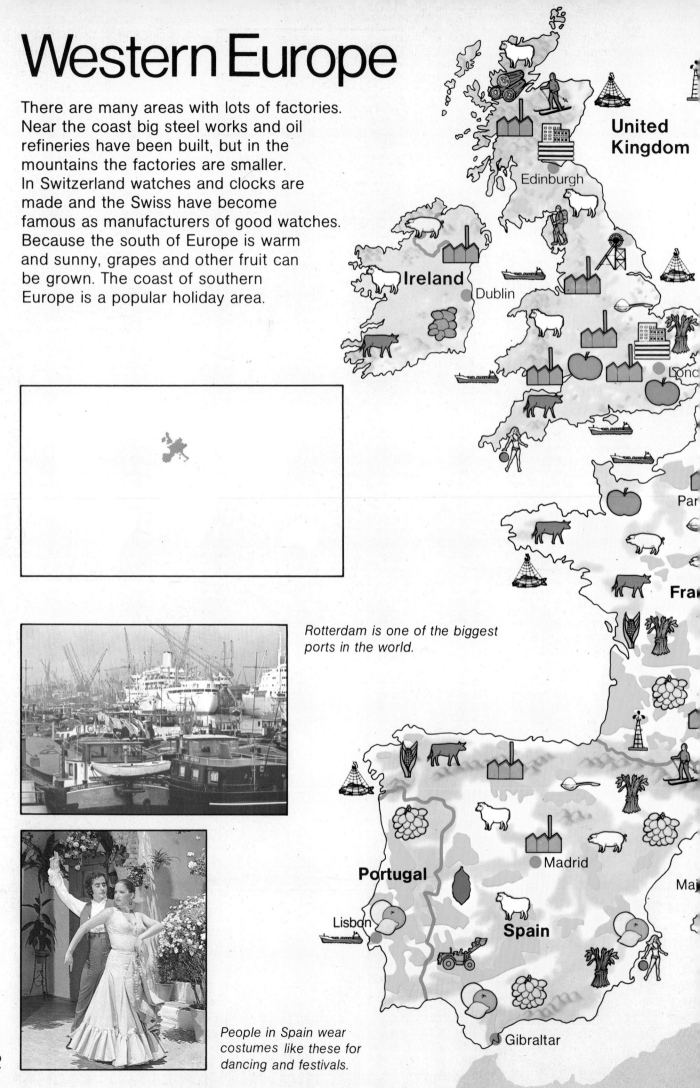

Rotterdam is one of the biggest ports in the world.

People in Spain wear costumes like these for dancing and festivals.

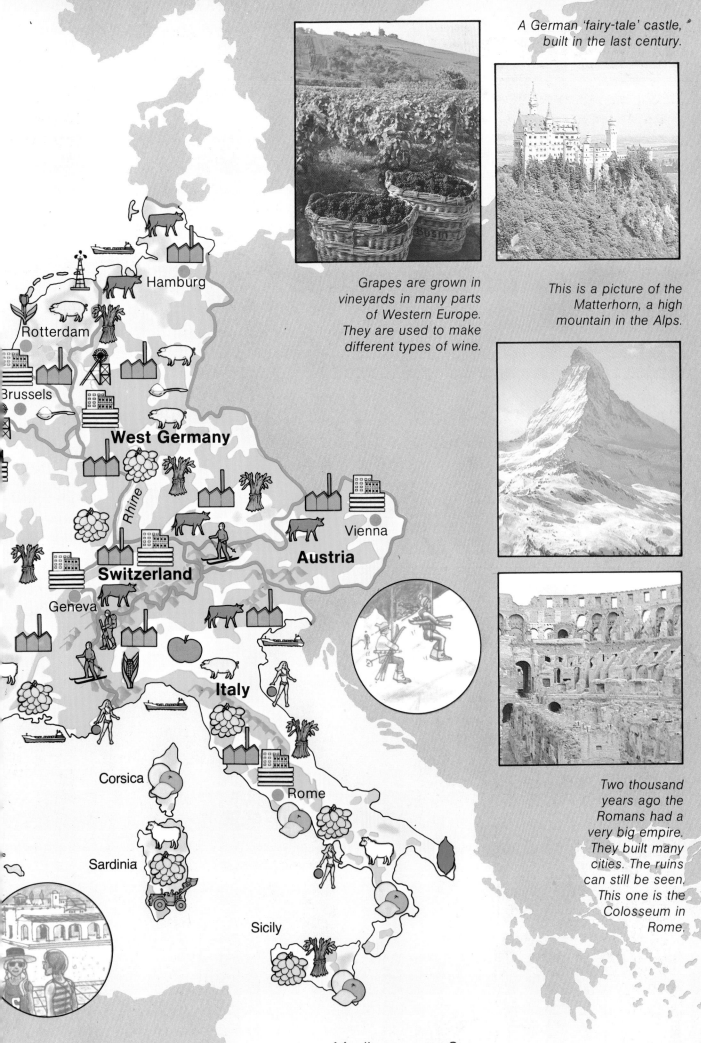

A German 'fairy-tale' castle, built in the last century.

Grapes are grown in vineyards in many parts of Western Europe. They are used to make different types of wine.

This is a picture of the Matterhorn, a high mountain in the Alps.

Two thousand years ago the Romans had a very big empire. They built many cities. The ruins can still be seen. This one is the Colosseum in Rome.

Hamburg

Rotterdam

Brussels

West Germany

Rhine

Vienna

Austria

Switzerland

Geneva

Italy

Corsica

Rome

Sardinia

Sicily

Mediterranean Sea

Eastern Europe

The river shown on the map is the Danube. Boats travel along this river carrying goods to countries in Eastern and Western Europe.

In the cities of Eastern Europe there are many large factories and housing estates owned by the government. In the countryside peasant farmers live in villages which have not changed much for hundreds of years.

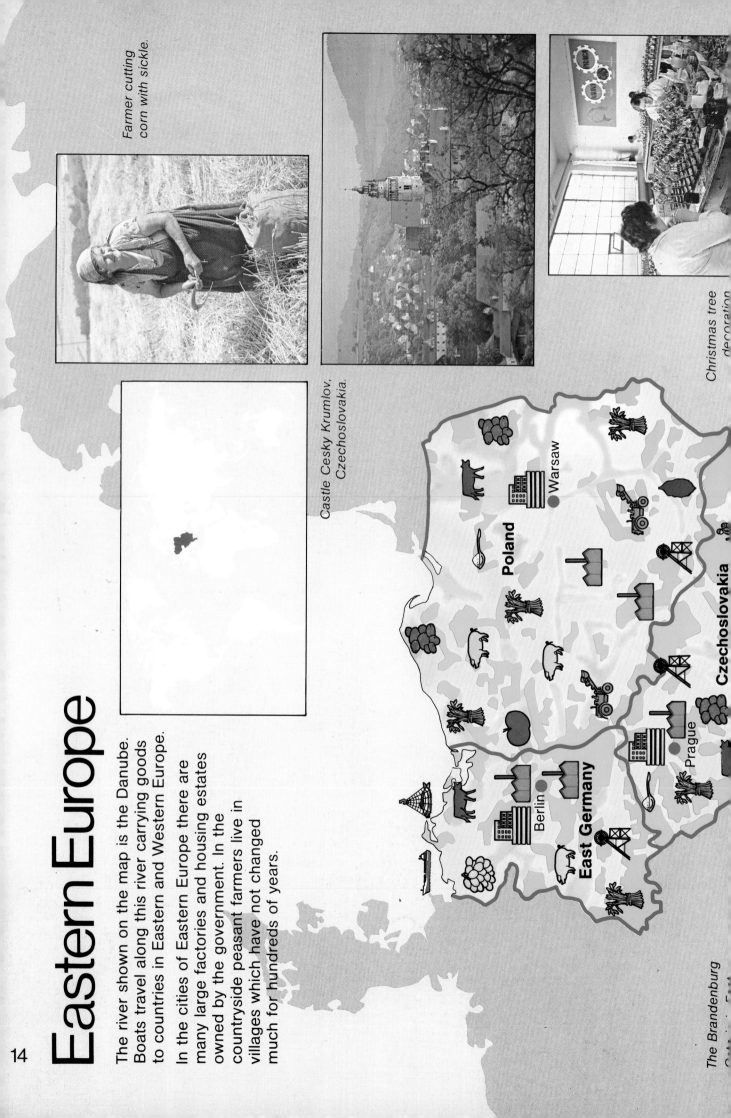

Farmer cutting corn with sickle.

Castle Cesky Krumlov, Czechoslovakia.

Christmas tree decoration

The Brandenburg

Poland

Warsaw

East Germany

Berlin

Prague

Czechoslovakia

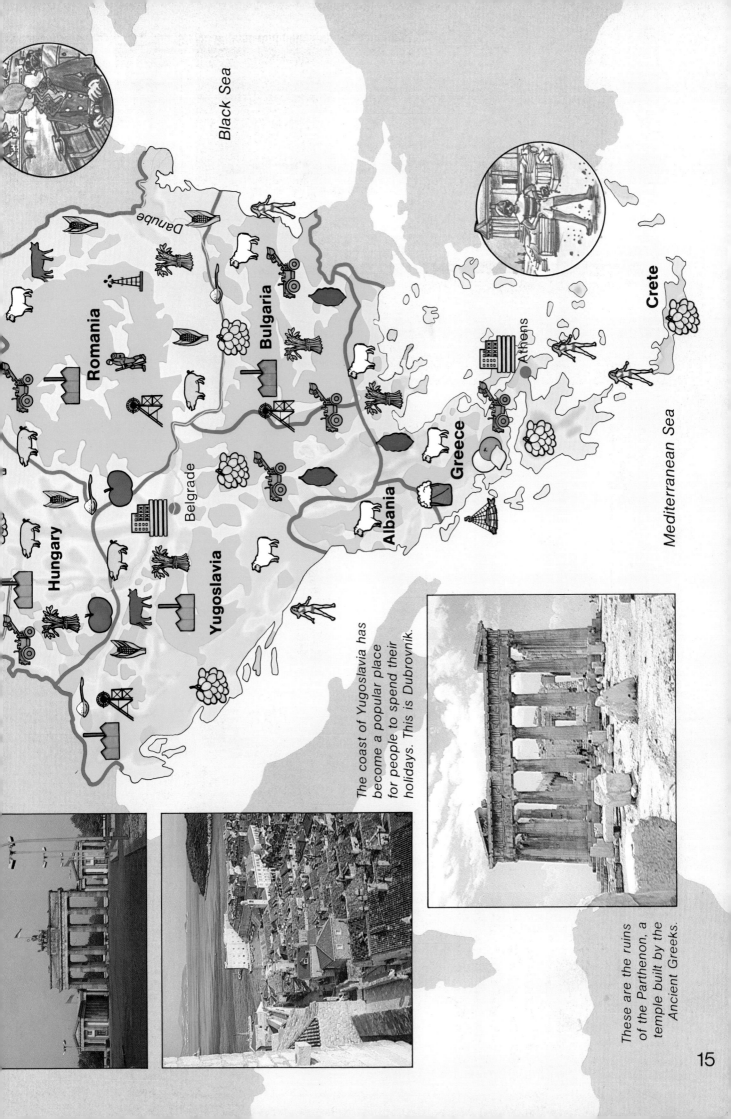

Black Sea

Danube

Romania

Bulgaria

Belgrade

Hungary

Yugoslavia

Albania

Greece

Athens

Crete

Mediterranean Sea

The coast of Yugoslavia has become a popular place for people to spend their holidays. This is Dubrovnik.

These are the ruins of the Parthenon, a temple built by the Ancient Greeks.

Scandinavia

Most of the land is covered with forests, lakes, and mountains. In the North it is called "The Land of the Midnight Sun". This is because in summer the sun shines all through the night. In winter it is dark all through the day. The farmers in Denmark sell butter and bacon to other countries.

The people in Sweden make paper from their trees for other countries. Most people live in the South, where there are farms, factories, and towns.

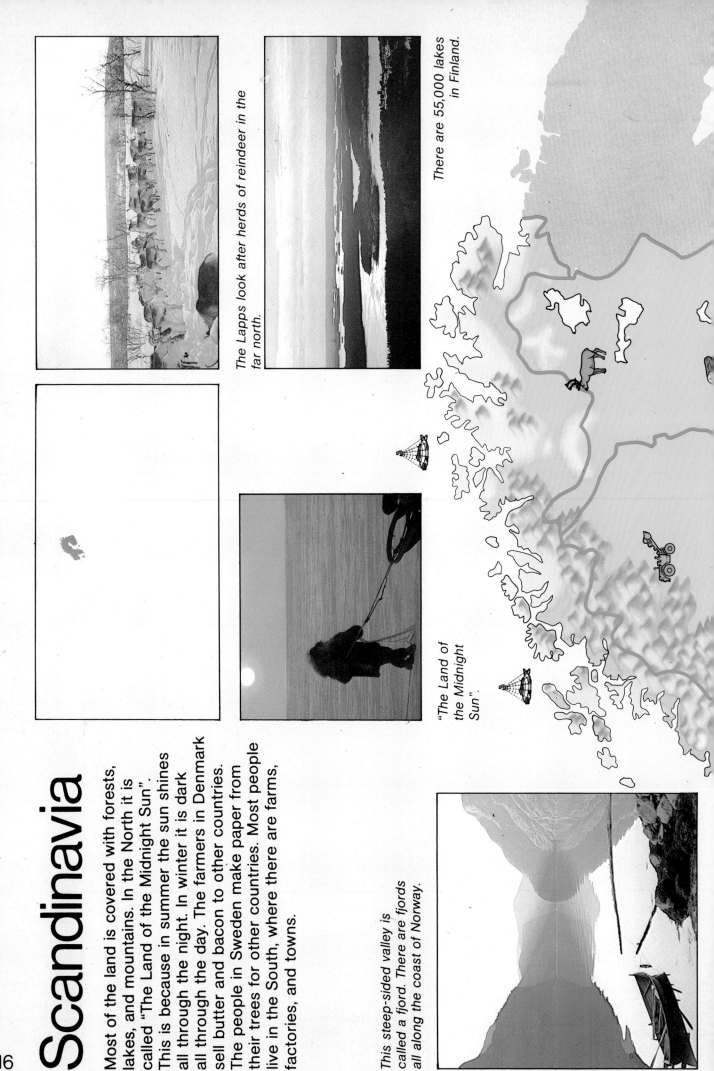

The Lapps look after herds of reindeer in the far north.

There are 55,000 lakes in Finland.

"The Land of the Midnight Sun".

This steep-sided valley is called a fjord. There are fjords all along the coast of Norway.

This is part of the city of Stockholm. The view was taken from the roof of the City Hall.

The Little Mermaid watches over the port of Copenhagen. It is a famous landmark.

Finland

Helsinki

Sweden

Stockholm

Norway

Oslo

Gothenburg

Copenhagen

Denmark

Russia

Russia is the biggest country in the world. Most people live in the western part where there are very large farms and factories. The government is trying to get more people to move to new towns in Siberia, the eastern part of Russia. The great forest is known as the Taiga. It is shaded green on the map. The forest stretches right across Russia.

Leningrad

Moscow

Volga

Black Sea

Caspian Sea

This monastery is in Georgia, a province near the Black Sea.

At the Kosmos Centre in Moscow we can see how the Russian people have used science to change and develop their lives.

18

Large areas of flat grassland in Russia are known as Steppes.

Siberia

Vladivostok

This village is by Lake Baikal, in Siberia.

This is the Moskvich car factory in Moscow.

From the River Moskva we can see the centre of the capital city of Russia, Moscow and its government building, the Kremlin.

Canada

There is tundra in northern Canada, in an area where it is too cold for trees to grow. In winter the land is covered with snow and ice but in the summer most of the ice melts and small plants grow everywhere in the wet ground. Not many people live in the tundra or the great forests. The cities and farms are further south where it is warmer.

Alaska
(U.S.A.)

Mackenzie

Vancouver

The mountain scenery in Canada is very beautiful. These are the Rocky Mountains.

These men who are sawing the trees down are called lumberjacks. The trees will be made into paper. Strong machinery is used to lift the trees on to huge transporters.

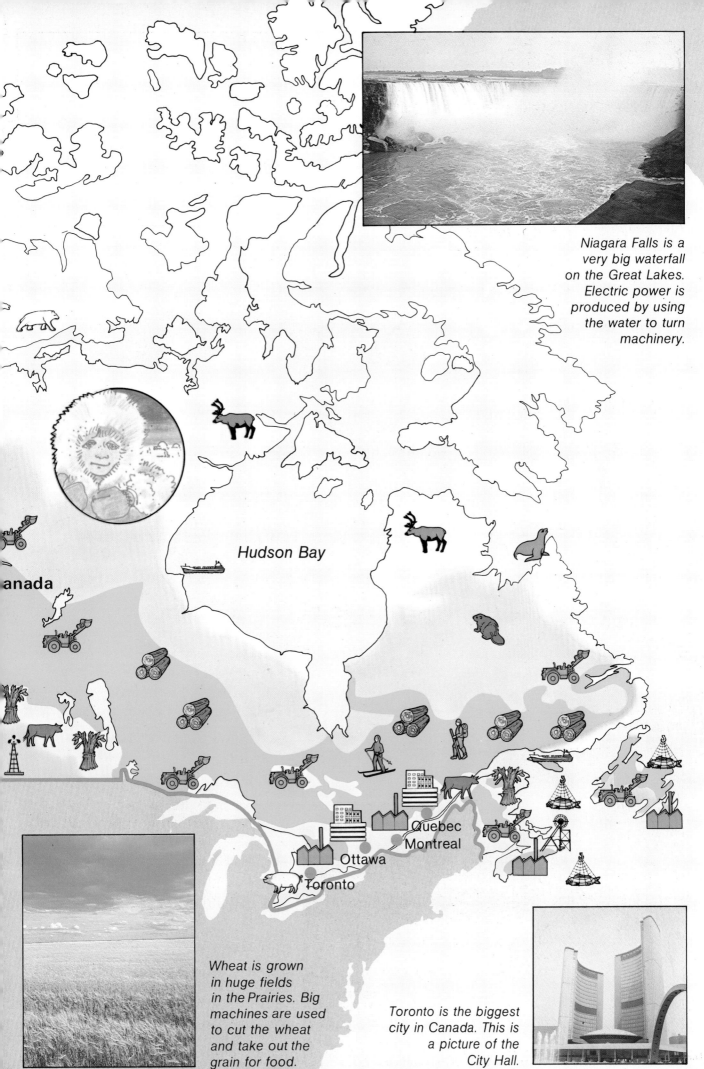

Niagara Falls is a very big waterfall on the Great Lakes. Electric power is produced by using the water to turn machinery.

Hudson Bay

anada

Quebec
Montreal

Ottawa

Toronto

Wheat is grown in huge fields in the Prairies. Big machines are used to cut the wheat and take out the grain for food.

Toronto is the biggest city in Canada. This is a picture of the City Hall.

United States of America

Indian tribes once wandered freely all over what is now called the United States. Then other people came to live in America from many different parts of the world. Today, the United States has modern farms, big cities, and many different kinds of industry.

Many cities have very tall buildings called sky-scrapers, where people work in offices. The buildings are tall because land in the cities costs a lot of money so it is cheaper to build upwards than outwards.

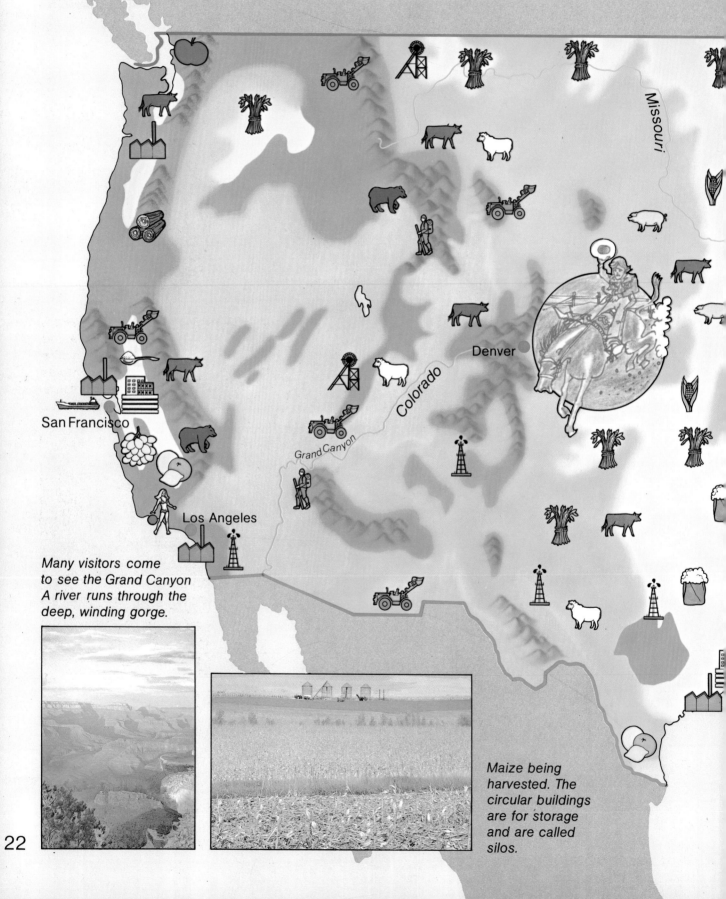

San Francisco

Los Angeles

Denver

Colorado

Grand Canyon

Missouri

Many visitors come to see the Grand Canyon A river runs through the deep, winding gorge.

Maize being harvested. The circular buildings are for storage and are called silos.

22

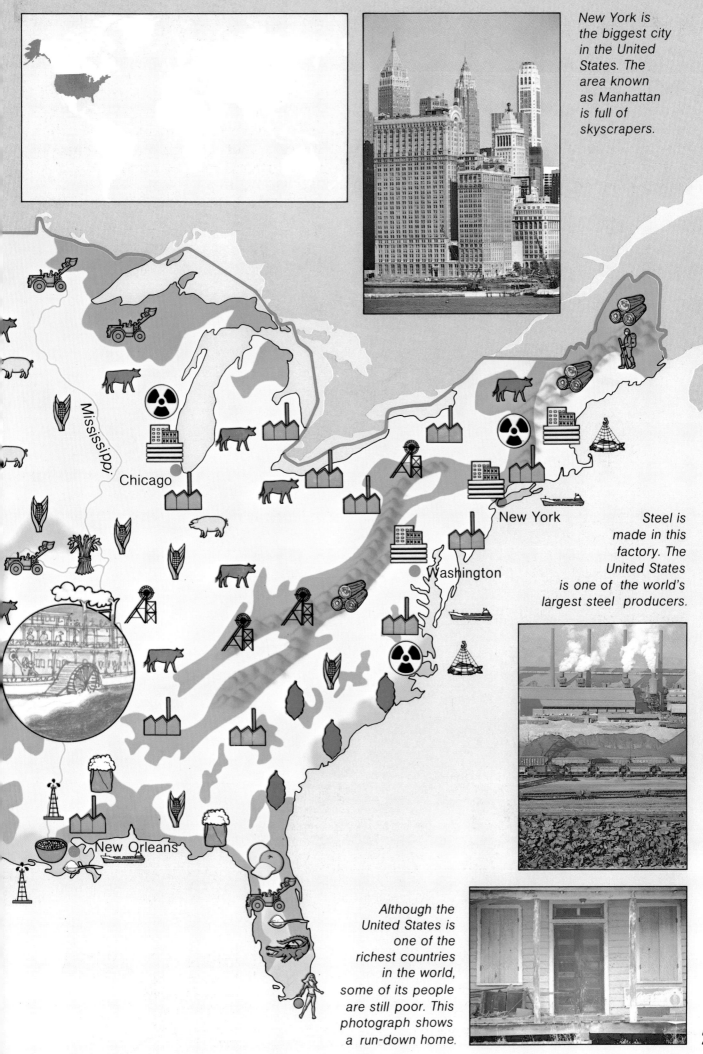

New York is the biggest city in the United States. The area known as Manhattan is full of skyscrapers.

Mississippi

Chicago

New York

Washington

New Orleans

Steel is made in this factory. The United States is one of the world's largest steel producers.

Although the United States is one of the richest countries in the world, some of its people are still poor. This photograph shows a run-down home.

23

Central America

In Central America there are high, dry mountains and wet, tropical jungles. Most people work on farms. Sugar cane and bananas are grown nearly everywhere. In the Caribbean Sea there are many tropical islands with palm trees along the shore. Brightly coloured fish live around the coral reefs in the sea. Can you find the Panama Canal on the map? It is used by big ships to cross from one ocean to another.

Mexico

Mexico City

Guatemala

Many centuries ago the Indians built temples and made beautiful objects from silver. This is an ancient temple.

A Sunday market.

Bananas grow in big bunches. Most of them are sold to other countries. When they are shipped they are green, but ripen on the journey to a bright yellow colour.

24

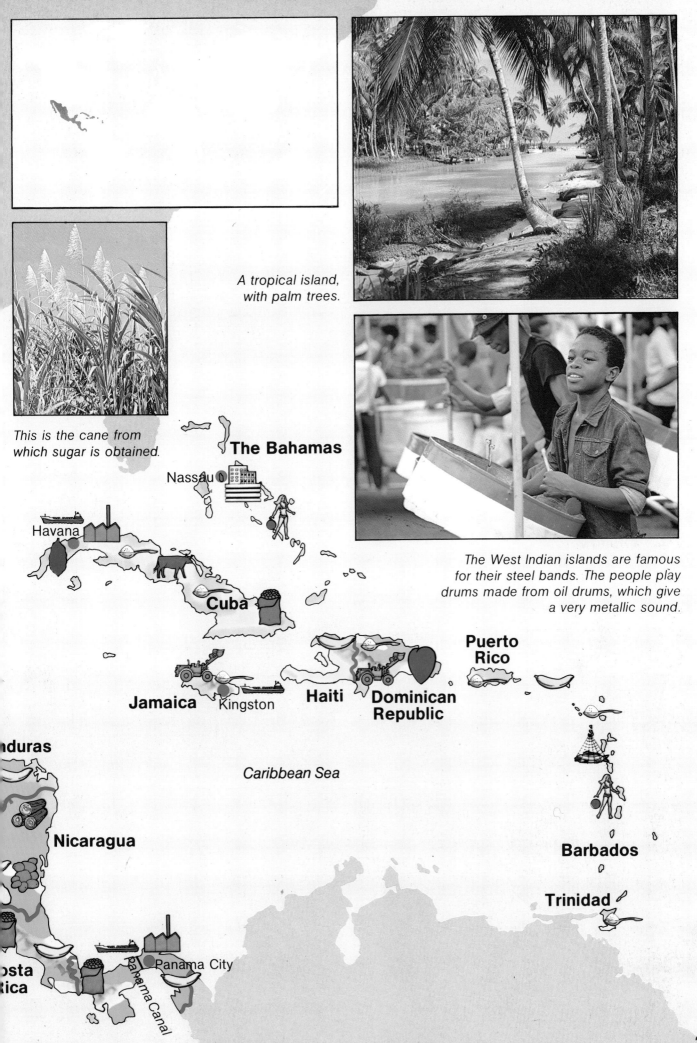

A tropical island, with palm trees.

This is the cane from which sugar is obtained.

The West Indian islands are famous for their steel bands. The people play drums made from oil drums, which give a very metallic sound.

The Bahamas

Nassau

Havana

Cuba

Jamaica
Kingston

Haiti

Dominican Republic

Puerto Rico

Caribbean Sea

nduras

Nicaragua

Barbados

Trinidad

osta Rica

Panama City

Panama Canal

South America

The inland part of Brazil is covered by a huge tropical forest. It rains nearly every day and the trees grow very tall and close together. Hardly any sunlight reaches the ground. Long creepers called lianas stretch from tree to tree. Some people in South America own big farms and are very wealthy, but most people are poor and have to work hard to get enough to eat.

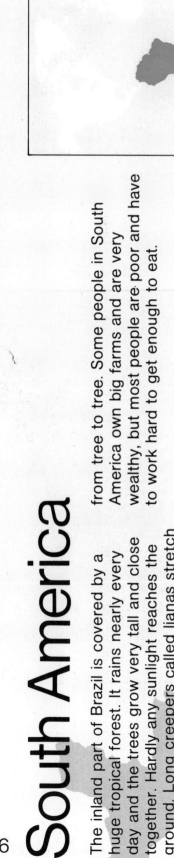

Caracas

Venezuela

Colombia

Ecuador

Peru

Amazon

Lima

Brazil

Bolivia

New roads and towns are being built where there was once only thick jungle and small Indian villages.

Indians in the tropical rain forest use blow-pipes to shoot small animals and birds for food.

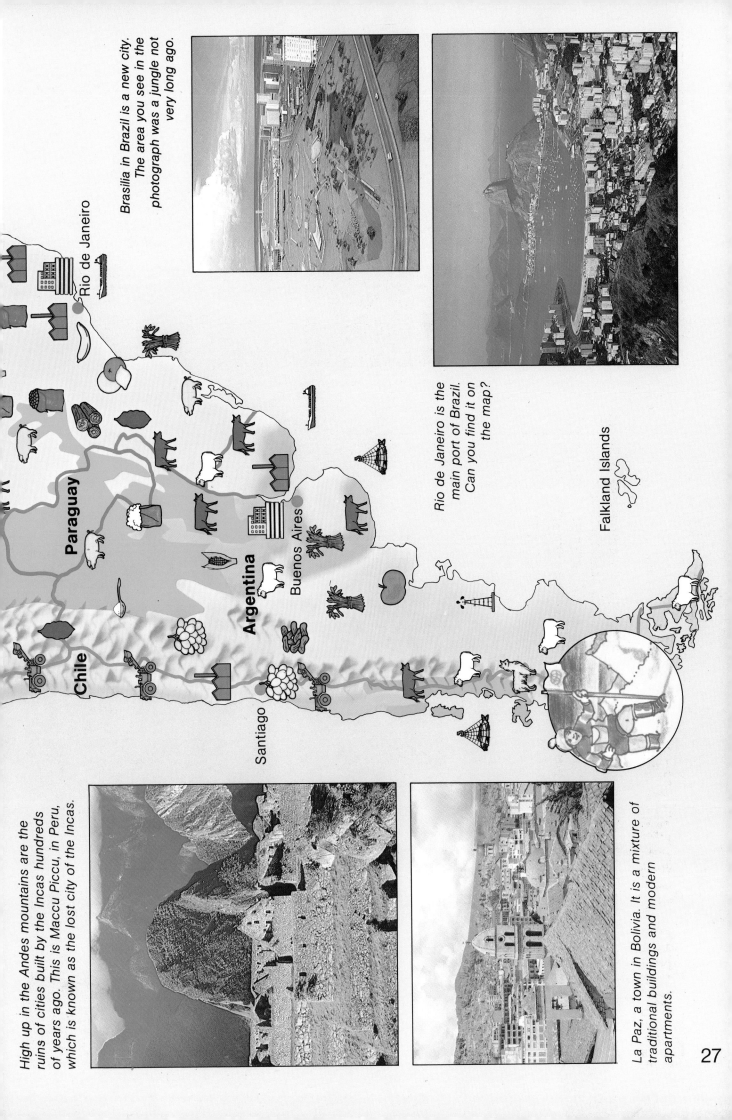

Brasilia in Brazil is a new city. The area you see in the photograph was a jungle not very long ago.

Rio de Janeiro

Rio de Janeiro is the main port of Brazil. Can you find it on the map?

Falkland Islands

Paraguay

Chile

Argentina

Buenos Aires

Santiago

High up in the Andes mountains are the ruins of cities built by the Incas hundreds of years ago. This is Maccu Piccu, in Peru, which is known as the lost city of the Incas.

La Paz, a town in Bolivia. It is a mixture of traditional buildings and modern apartments.

27

Africa

There are many different countries in Africa. Some are big and others very small. Some countries are rich and others are poor. Most of them used to be ruled by people from other countries, like Britain and France, but now they are ruled by their own people. The Sahara in North Africa is the largest dry area of land in the world. It is 5,000 kilometres from one end to the other.

In the desert there are some places where water can be found, often in small pools. Around these pools, plants and palm trees can grow.

Oil tankers and other big ships can go through the Suez Canal. This can make their journey shorter.

These elephants live in a special park in Uganda where they are protected from hunters. Can you find some wild animals on the map?

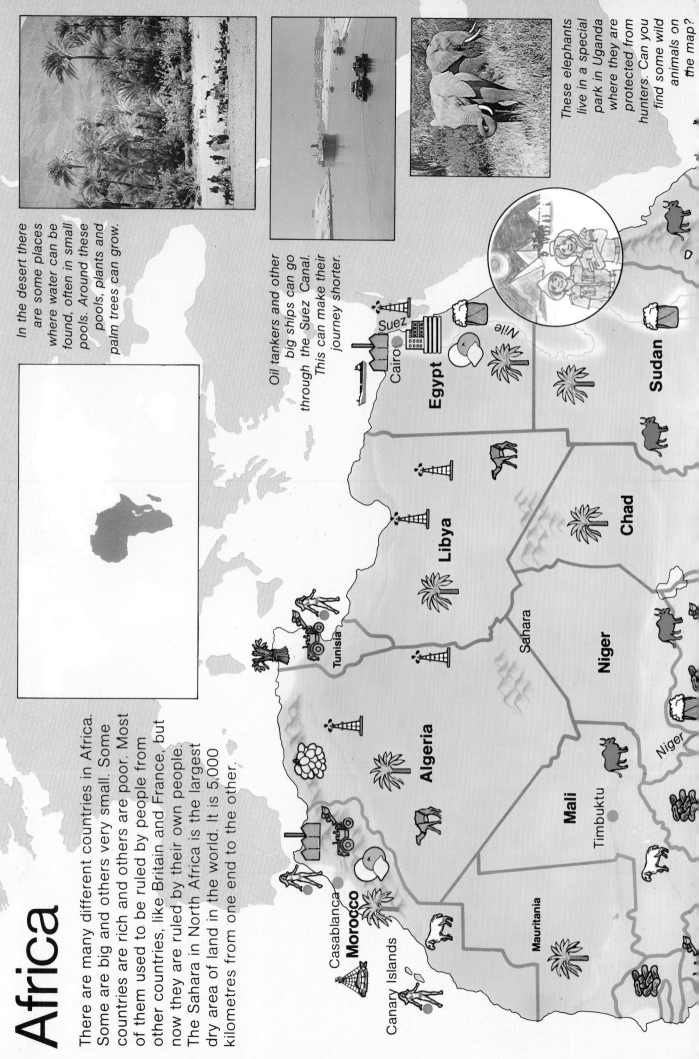

Canary Islands

Casablanca
Morocco

Mauritania

Algeria

Tunisia

Libya

Sahara

Mali

Timbuktu

Niger

Niger

Chad

Egypt

Cairo

Suez

Nile

Sudan

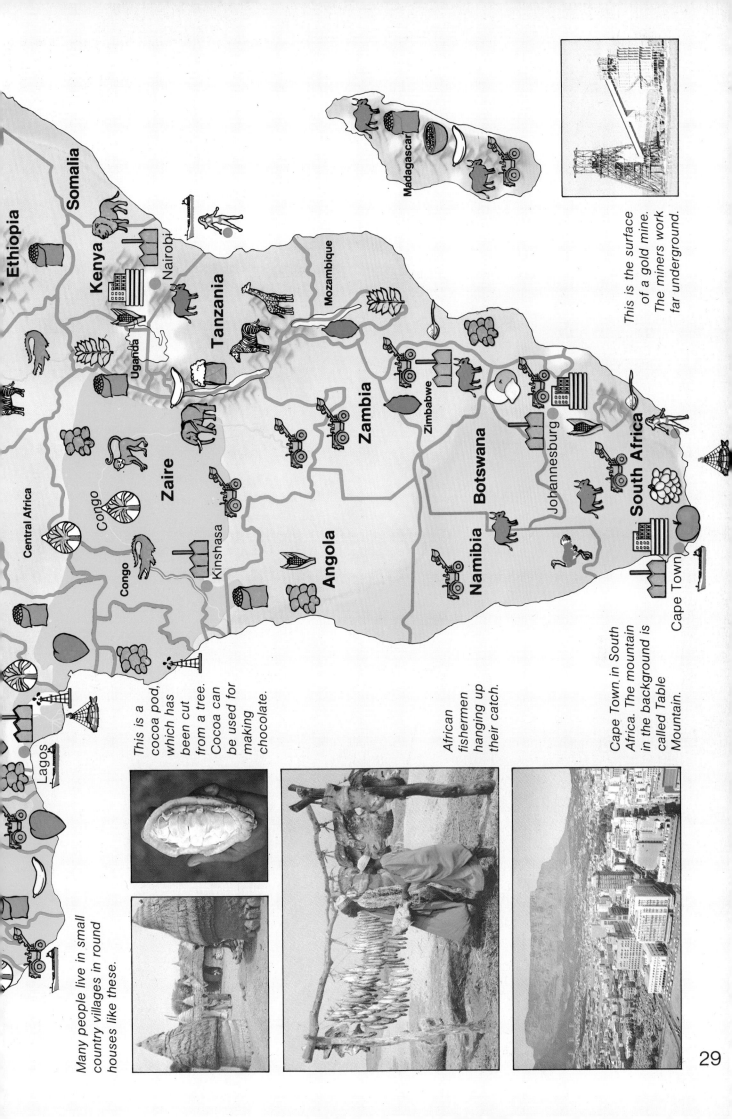

Ethiopia

Somalia

Kenya

Nairobi

Uganda

Tanzania

Zaire

Congo

Congo

Kinshasa

Central Africa

Lagos

Angola

Zambia

Mozambique

Madagascar

Zimbabwe

Botswana

Johannesburg

Namibia

South Africa

Cape Town

This is the surface of a gold mine. The miners work far underground.

This is a cocoa pod, which has been cut from a tree. Cocoa can be used for making chocolate.

African fishermen hanging up their catch.

Cape Town in South Africa. The mountain in the background is called Table Mountain.

Many people live in small country villages in round houses like these.

Middle East

A lot of the world's oil comes from the Middle East. Most of the land is very dry. In daytime it is hot, but at night it becomes cold. Some of the people who live in this area are nomads, and travel in the desert with their camels. The Holy Cities of Jerusalem and Mecca are in the Middle East. Can you find them on the map?

Istanbul

Turkey

Cyprus

Lebanon

Israel
Jerusalem

Mediterranean Sea

Syri

Jord

Red Sea

A street in Jerusalem. The sheepskin coats and rugs are for sale.

Omani tribesmen resting, their heads protected from the fierce sun by turbans.

A Jebali family. These nomads live in sturdy tents that can protect them from the heat of the day and the cold of the night.

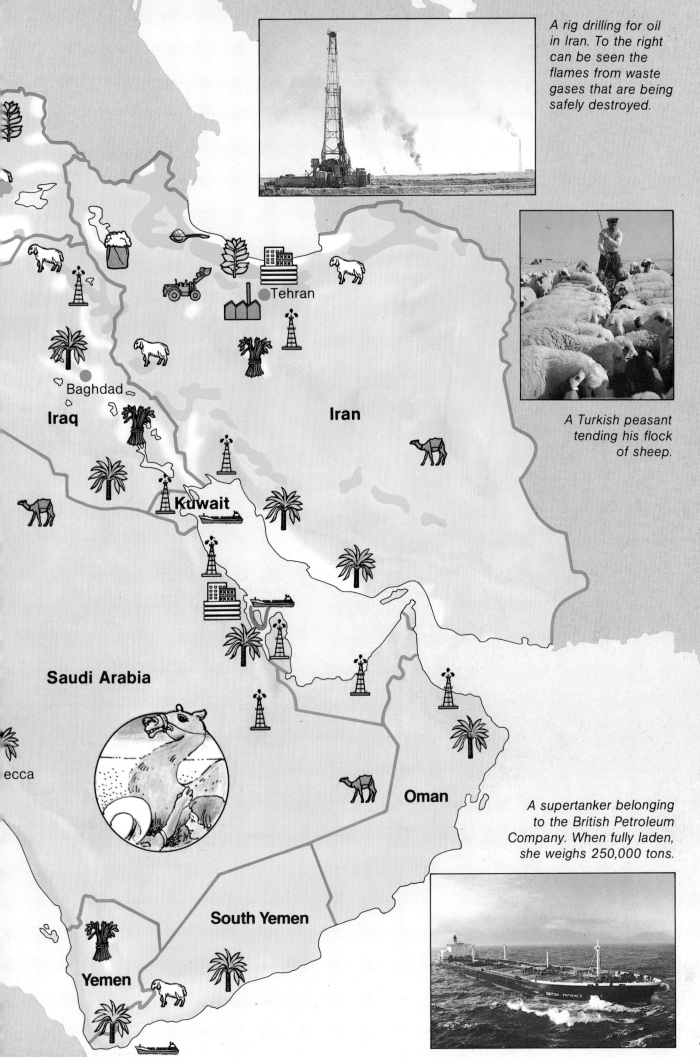

A rig drilling for oil in Iran. To the right can be seen the flames from waste gases that are being safely destroyed.

A Turkish peasant tending his flock of sheep.

Tehran

Iran

Iraq

Baghdad

Kuwait

Saudi Arabia

ecca

Oman

South Yemen

Yemen

A supertanker belonging to the British Petroleum Company. When fully laden, she weighs 250,000 tons.

India

This is an area of high mountains and wide valleys. Can you find Mount Everest on the map? It is the highest place on earth.

For long periods there is no rain at all and the crops die. Sometimes there are terrible floods which destroy houses and farms. Many people do not have enough to eat. In the cities there are some modern factories and new buildings, as well as beautiful temples and old palaces. Most people can only afford to live in small, shabby houses.

The Taj Mahal is a palace built by a great Prince. It is built of white marble inlaid with jewels.

Mount Everest is the highest mountain in the world.

Mount Everest

Nepal

Delhi

Afghanistan

Pakistan

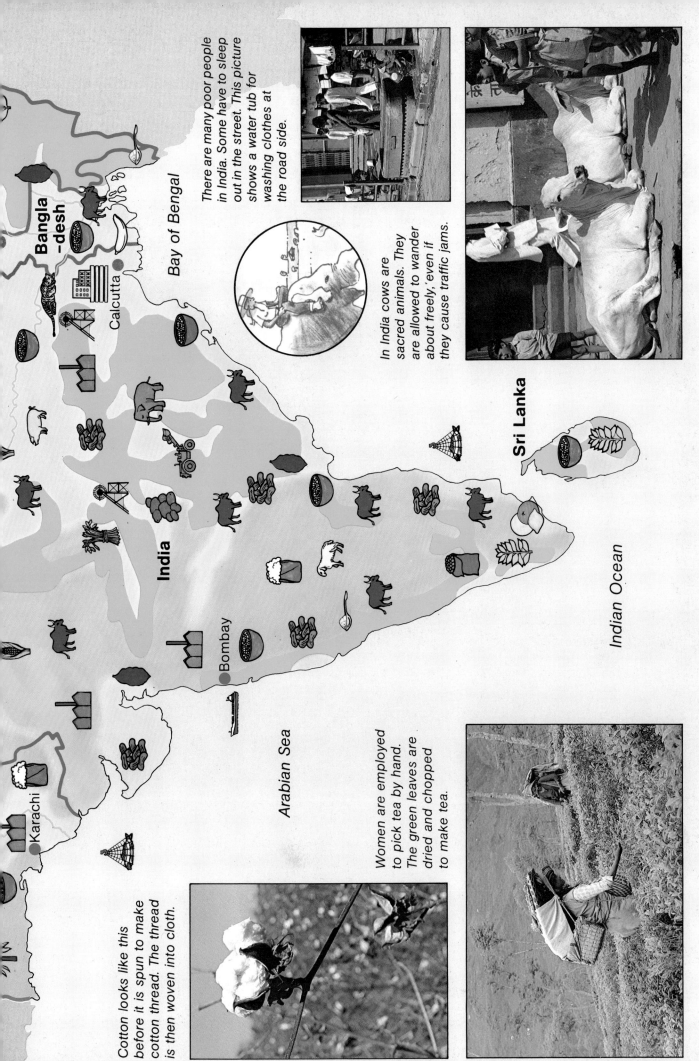

Bangla -desh

Bay of Bengal

Calcutta

There are many poor people in India. Some have to sleep out in the street. This picture shows a water tub for washing clothes at the road side.

In India cows are sacred animals. They are allowed to wander about freely, even if they cause traffic jams.

India

Bombay

Sri Lanka

Indian Ocean

Arabian Sea

Karachi

Women are employed to pick tea by hand. The green leaves are dried and chopped to make tea.

Cotton looks like this before it is spun to make cotton thread. The thread is then woven into cloth.

33

China

More people live in China than in any other country in the world. Most of them live in the countryside and work together in the fields or in small factories. Rice is their main food. It needs a lot of water to grow, so the rivers are used to irrigate the fields.

Mongolia

GREAT WALL

China

H

Chinese women washing clothes.

These fields are flooded to grow rice. They are called paddy fields.

34

Many people work together to dig up rocks and to build dams that control the rivers.

In this junior school in China, the children are writing the Chinese alphabet.

Peking

North Korea

South Korea

Shanghai

gtze Kiang

Taiwan

Hong Kong

This temple is in Peking, China.

The Great Wall was built a very long time ago to protect the Chinese from their enemies.

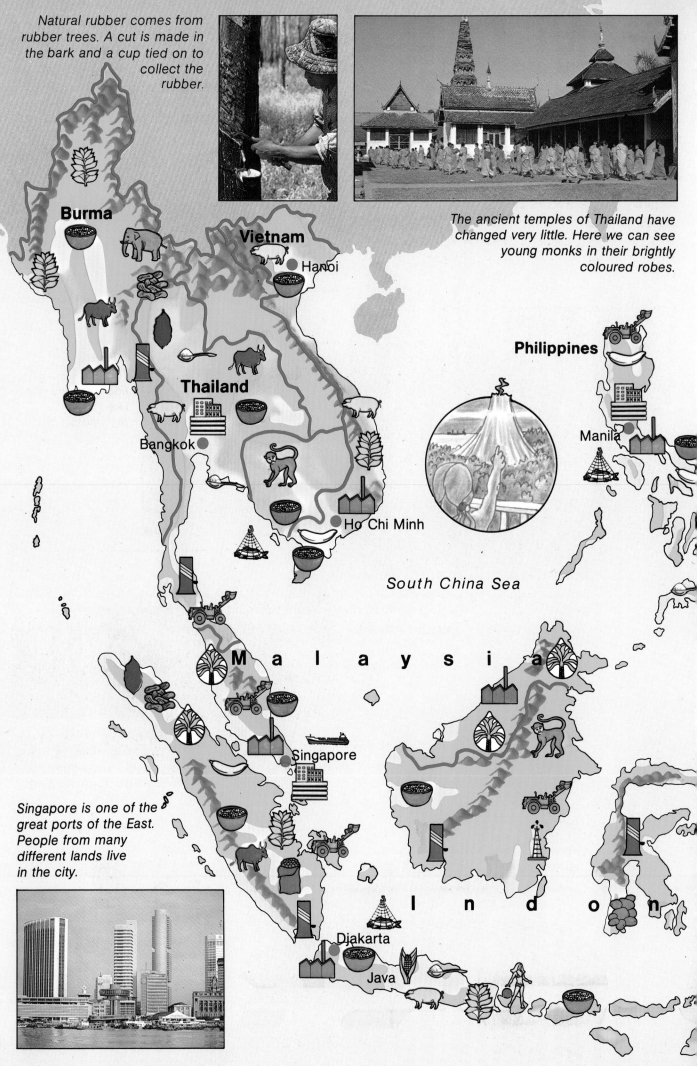

Natural rubber comes from rubber trees. A cut is made in the bark and a cup tied on to collect the rubber.

The ancient temples of Thailand have changed very little. Here we can see young monks in their brightly coloured robes.

Burma

Vietnam

Hanoi

Thailand

Bangkok

Philippines

Manila

Ho Chi Minh

South China Sea

M a l a y s i a

Singapore

Singapore is one of the great ports of the East. People from many different lands live in the city.

I n d o n e s i a

Djakarta

Java

South-East Asia

Most of South-East Asia is covered with tropical rain forest. Hundreds of years ago, traders came from Europe and took back home precious oils and spices. They called these islands the East Indies. Today, there are many very big cities in South-East Asia. Millions of people leave the countryside and move to the cities to find jobs. Can you find the island of Java on the map? It is one of the most densely populated islands in the world.

The islands are crowded with people and some live in boats on the water.
They buy food at floating markets, like this one in the photograph.

Where the land is hilly, rice is grown on fields which are cut into the hillsides.

In the big cities, many people are very poor and live in shanties. These are houses made of old scraps of wood and other things from rubbish dumps.

Pacific Ocean

s i a

New Guinea

Japan

The Japanese factories make radios, calculators, automobiles, motor bikes, and toys. Because there are a lot of factories it is very difficult to keep the air and the rivers clean and free from smoke and dust. Japan also has a very large number of shipyards and builds more ships than any other country.

At this Japanese port cuttlefish have been hung up to dry.

This colourful food store is in Tokyo. As you can see from the shop-sign Japanese writing is very different from our own.

Tokyo

Osaka

Mount Fuji is a volcano. It is quite near Tokyo and people often go to visit it.

New Zealand

New Zealand sends wool, meat, and butter to other countries. In the North Island there are volcanoes and geysers. A geyser is a hot water fountain.

These people are Maoris. Maoris lived in New Zealand long before European explorers discovered their country. They used to wear clothes like this all the time, but now they only dress up for special occasions.

Auckland

Wellington

Christchurch

Mount Cook is the highest mountain in New Zealand. There are many mountains and glaciers in the South Island.

This is a geyser. The water is very hot, as you can see from the steam coming off it.

Australia

The first people in Australia were the Aborigines. Now they have land in only a few parts of Australia. Australia is a rich country. There are large farms and mines. Nearly all the people live in towns and cities on the coast. The middle of Australia is very dry and not many people live there.

Only a few Aborigines still appear like this. Most of them wear modern clothes and live in towns.

Perth

Wool from sheep is an important product of Australian farms.

Big new mines are being dug in Australia, far away from any cities. This one will provide ore for making iron.

The Great Barrier Reef is made of coral. Coral is formed from the shell skeletons of millions of small sea animals.

GREAT BARRIER REEF

Alice Springs

Darling

Murray

Melbourne

Sydney

Canberra

A white wallaby with a baby in its pouch.

Sydney is the biggest city in Australia. Very large ships can come into the harbour. In this photograph you can see the Harbour Bridge and, to the left of it, the Opera House.

41

North Pole

If Simon and Sarah were to get on a space-ship and orbit the Earth, they would see that the Earth is round. At the extreme northern end of the Earth is the North Pole, where the sea is frozen to form a solid ice cap.

Canada

Russia

Greenland

Iceland

Scandinavia

This is the tip of an iceberg.
Most of it floats under the cold water.

A team of Husky dogs
pulls travellers over snow and ice.

South Pole

At the other end of the Earth, Simon and Sarah would see the South Pole and the frozen continent of Antarctica, as they flew over in their space-ship.

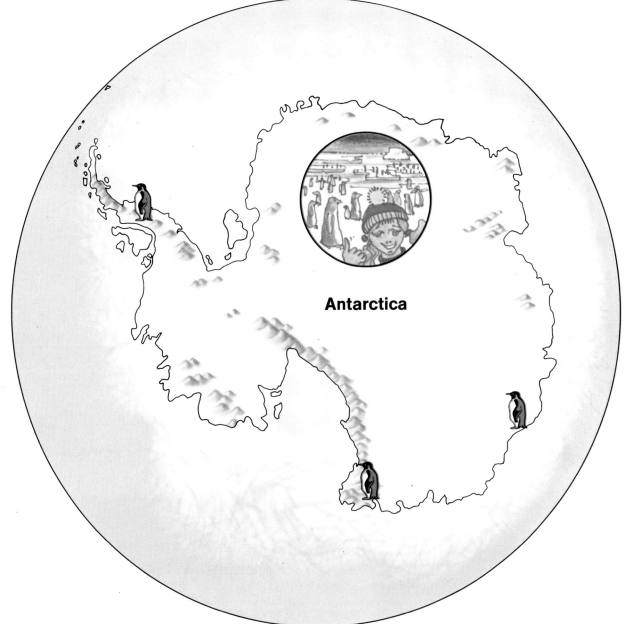

Antarctica

Flat-footed birds called Penguins have their home at the South Pole.

People from many countries visit Antarctica to carry out scientific work.

The World from Space

Looking at the world from space, Simon and Sarah would see the continents partly covered by clouds, as in this photograph taken by a satellite going around the Earth. Can you see which part of the world is shown on the photograph? The area of the Earth which is turned away from the sun is in darkness. The world spins round in space every day and there is always one half of our planet where it is night, and one half where it is day.

The planets and the Earth move around the sun.

MERCURY

VENUS

EARTH

MARS

JUPITER

SATURN

URANUS

NEPTUNE

MOON

As the Earth travels through space around the Sun, so the Moon travels around the Earth.

PLUTO

The Ages of Life on Earth

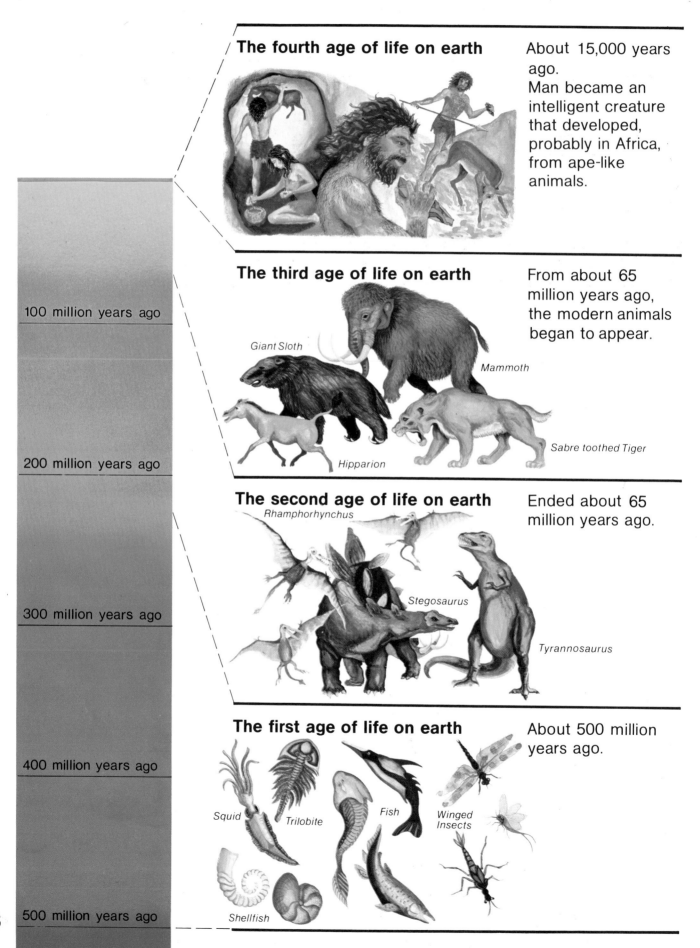

100 million years ago

200 million years ago

300 million years ago

400 million years ago

500 million years ago

The fourth age of life on earth

About 15,000 years ago.
Man became an intelligent creature that developed, probably in Africa, from ape-like animals.

The third age of life on earth

From about 65 million years ago, the modern animals began to appear.

Giant Sloth

Mammoth

Sabre toothed Tiger

Hipparion

The second age of life on earth

Ended about 65 million years ago.

Rhamphorhynchus

Stegosaurus

Tyrannosaurus

The first age of life on earth

About 500 million years ago.

Squid

Trilobite

Fish

Winged Insects

Shellfish